**McGraw·Hill**

New York   Chicago   San Francisco   Lisbon   London   Madrid   Mexico City
Milan   New Delhi   San Juan   Seoul   Singapore   Sydney   Toronto

# About this book

Jane Wightwick
had the idea

Wina Gunn
wrote the pages

Leila Gaafar (aged 10)
drew the first pictures in
each chapter

Robert Bowers
(not aged 10) drew the
other pictures, and
designed the book

Ana Bremon

did the Spanish stuff

Important things that **must** be included

First published in the United States in 2001 by

McGraw-Hill
Two Penn Plaza
New York
NY 10121
U.S.A.

McGraw-Hill books are available at special quantity
discounts to use as premiums and sales promotions,
or for use in training programs. For more information,
please write to the Director of Special Sales, Professional
Publishing, McGraw-Hill, Two Penn Plaza, New York, NY
10121-2298. Or contact your local bookstore.

Printed in Singapore

Library of Congress Catalog Card Number: 00-135722

International Standard Book Number: 0-658-01691-1

05 06 07 08 09   15 14 13 12 11 10 9 8 7

# What's inside

## Making friends

How to be cool with the group

## Wanna play?

Our guide to joining in everything from hide-and-seek to the latest electronic game

## Feeling hungry

Order your favorite foods or go local

## Looking good

Make sure you keep up with all those essential fashions

## Hanging out

At the pool, beach, or theme park—don't miss out on the action

## Pocket money

Spend it here!

## Grown-up talk

blah! blah! blah! blah!

If you really, really have to!

## Extra stuff

All the handy things—numbers, months, dates, days of the week

MAKING FRIENDS

me
yo 👄 yo

my snake
mi serpiente
👄 mee serpee
entay

my friend
mi amigo
👄 mee ameego

my friend
mi amiga
👄 mee ameea

my dog
mi perro
👄 mee pair-ro

6

**my big brother**
mi hermano mayor
👄 mee airmano my-yor

**grandpa**
abuelo
👄 abwelo

**grandma**
abuela
👄 abwela

**dad**
papá
👄 pa-pah

**mom**
mamá
👄 ma-mah

**my little sister**
mi hermana pequeña
👄 mee airmana pekenya

## Half a step this way

**stepfather/stepmother**
padrastro/madrastra
👄 padrastro/madrastra

**half brother/half sister**
medio hermano/medio hermana
👄 medyo airmano/medyo airmana

**stepbrother/stepsister**
hermanastro/hermanastra
👄 airmanastro/airmanastra

7

In Spanish you put an upside-down question mark before a question, as well as one right-side-up at the end. It's the same with exclamation marks.

¿Isn't that weird?  ¡You bet!

8

Where are you from?
¿De dónde eres?
👄 day donday air-res

from Canada
de Canadá
👄 day canadah

from Ireland
de Irlanda
👄 day eerlanda

from Scotland
de Escocia
👄 day escosya

from Wales
del País de Gales
👄 del pie-yis day gal-les

from the U.S.
de los Estados Unidos
👄 day los estados
ooneedos

from England
de Inglaterra
👄 day eengla-tairra

9

How old are you?
¿Cuántos años tienes?
👄 kwantos anyos tee-enes

12 years old
Doce años
👄 dosay anyos

Happy birthday!
¡Cumpleaños feliz!
👄 koomplay-anyos faileess

What's your star sign?
¿Qué signo del zodiaco eres?
👄 kay signo del sodee-ako air-res

When's your birthday?
¿Cuándo es tu cumpleaños?
👄 kwando es too koomplay-anyos

Children sing "Happy Birthday" in Spanish to the same tune. Why don't you practice:

¡Cumpleaños Feliz!
¡Cumpleaños Feliz!

10

# Star Signs

**AQUARIUS**
Jan. 21 – Feb. 19
Acuario — akwaree-o

**PISCES**
Feb. 20 – Mar. 20
Piscis — pees-sees

**ARIES**
Mar. 21 – Apr. 20
Aries — a-rees

**TAURUS**
Apr. 21 – May 21
Tauro — touro

**GEMINI**
May 22 – June 21
Géminis — hemeenees

**CANCER**
June 22 – July 23
Cáncer — kansair

**LEO**
July 24 – Aug. 23
Leo — leo

**VIRGO**
Aug. 24 – Sep. 23
Virgo — beergo

**LIBRA**
Sep. 24 – Oct. 23
Libra — leebra

**SCORPIO**
Oct. 24 – Nov. 22
Escorpio — eskorpee-o

**SAGITTARIUS**
Nov. 23 – Dec. 21
Sagitario — sa-heetaree-o

**CAPRICORN**
Dec. 22 – Jan. 20
Capricornio — kapreecornee

11

**soccer**
el fútbol
👄 el footbol

**rollerskating/rollerblading**
el patinaje en línea
👄 el patee-nahay en leenya

**music**
la música
👄 la mooseeka

**electronic games**
los juegos electrónicos
👄 los hway-gos elektroneekos

**tv**
la tele
👄 la taylay

**comics**
los tebeos
👄 los taybayos

**teddy bears**
los ositos de peluche
👄 los oseetos day peloochay

**school**
el colegio
👄 el kolay-heeyo

**spiders**
las arañas
👄 las aranyas

13

What's your ...?
¿Cuál es tu ... ?
☞ kwal es too ...

favorite group
grupo preferido
☞ groopo prefereedo

favorite color
color preferido
☞ kol-lor prefereedo

Page 51

favorite food
comida preferida
☞ komeeda prefereeda

favorite team
equipo preferido
☞ ekeepo prefereedo

favorite animal
animal preferido
☞ anee-mal prefereedo

cat
el gato
👄 el gato

dog
el perro
👄 el pair-ro

snake
la serpiente
👄 la serpee-entay

guinea pig
la cobaya
👄 la kob-eye-a

hamster
el hámster
👄 el ahmstair

parakeet
el periquito
👄 el peree-keeto

## My little doggy goes *guau guau!*

A doggy (that's "guauguau" in baby language) doesn't say "woof, woof" in Spanish; it says *"guau, guau"* (*gwa-oo, gwa-oo*). A Spanish bird says *"pío, pío"* (*pee-o, pee-o*) and "cock-a-doodle-do" in Spanish chicken-speak is *"kikirikí"* (*kee-kee ree-kee*). But a cat does say *"miaow"* and a cow *"moo"* whether they're speaking Spanish or English!

science
**las ciencias**
🔊 las see-en-see-as

history
**la historia**
🔊 la eestoreeya

## School rules!

In Spanish-speaking countries, many children have to wear a uniform to school, and discipline is quite strict. On the other hand, they enjoy long vacation breaks: about 10 weeks in the summer and another 5–6 weeks during the school year. But before you turn green with envy, you might not like the mounds of "**tareas para las vacaciones**" (*taray-ahs para las bakasee-yones*); that's "vacation 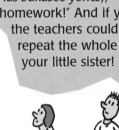 homework!" And if you fail your exams, the teachers could make you repeat the whole year with your little sister!

# Gossip

Can you keep a secret?

¡Puedes guardar un secreto?

👄 pwedes gwardar oon sekreto

Do you have a boyfriend (a girlfriend)?

¿Tienes novio (novia)?

👄 tee-enes nobyo (nobya)

An OK guy/An OK girl

Un chavo bueno/Una chava buena 👄 oon chabo bwayno/ oona chaba bwayna

Way bossy!

¡Qué mandón!

👄 kay man-don (boy)

¡Qué mandona!

👄 kay man-dona (girl)

He/She's nutty!

¡Está como una cabra!

👄 esta komo oona kabra

That means "He/She's like a goat!"

"I'm not like that at all!"

What a creep!

¡Qué malasombra!

👄 kay malas-sombra

18

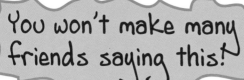

You won't make many friends saying this!

Bug off!
¡Vete a la porra!
⮑ betay a la porra

Shut up!
¡Cállate!
⮑ kigh-yatay

If you're fed up with someone, and you want to say something like "you silly …!" or "you stupid …!", you can start with **"pedazo de"** (which actually means "piece of …") and add anything you like. What about …

Stupid banana!
**¡Pedazo de plátano!**
(pedaso day platano)

or …

Silly sausage!
**¡Pedazo de salchicha!**
(pedaso day salcheecha)

Take your pick. It should do the trick. You could also try **"¡Pedazo de idiota!"** (pedaso day eedee-ota). You don't need a translation here, do you?

# You might have to say

Fudge!
¡Ostras!
👄 os-stras

Rats!
¡Porras!
👄 porras

"Did someone call us?"

las ostras

I'm fed up
¡Estoy harto! (boys)
¡Estoy harta! (girls)
👄 estoy arto
estoy arta

That's enough!
¡Ya basta!
👄 ya basta

I don't care
Me da igual
👄 may da eegwal

Stop!
¡Para!
👄 para

At last!
¡Por fin!
👄 por feen

# Saying good-bye

**Here's my address**
Aquí tienes mi dirección
akee tee-enes mee
deerek-syon

**What's your address?**
¿Cuál es tu dirección?
kwal es too deerek-syon

**Come to visit me**
Ven a visitarme
ben a
beesee-tarmay

**Write to me soon**
Escríbeme pronto
eskree-bemay pronto

**Have a good trip!**
¡Buen viaje!
bwen bee-ahay

**Bye!**
¡Adiós!
adeeyos

WANNA PLAY?

el elástico
el elasteeko

el ping-pong
el "ping-pong"

la pata coja
👄 la pata ko-ha

el Gameboy®
👄 el "gameboy"

las canicas
👄 las kaneekas

el yo-yó
👄 el "yo yo"

WANNA PLAY?

23

Do you want to play ...?

¿Quieres jugar ...?

👄 keyair-res hoogar

... foos-ball?

... al futbolín?

👄 al footboleen

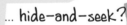

... cards?

... a las cartas?

👄 a las kartas

... on the computer?

... con la computadora?

👄 kon la kompootadora

... tic-tac-toe?

... a las tres en raya?

👄 a las trays en righ-ya

... hide-and-seek?

... al escondite?

👄 al eskon-deetay

... catch?

... al balón?

👄 al ballon

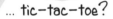

## Care for a game of **foal** or **donkey**?!

In Spain, you don't play "leap frog," you play "foal" —*el potro*. There is also a group version of this called "donkey"—*el burro*. This involves two teams. Team 1 lines up in a row with their heads down in the shape of a donkey. Team 2 takes turns to leap as far as they can onto the back of the "donkey." If the donkey falls over, Team 2 wins. If Team 2 touches the ground or can't leap far enough to get all the team on, then Team 1 wins—got that?! Spanish children will try to tell you this is enormous fun, but your parents might not be so happy about the bruises!

# Make yourself heard

You're it!
¡La quedas tú!
👄 la kedas too

Who's winning?
¿Quién gana?
👄 keeyen gana

Race you?
¿Una carrera?
👄 oona karraira

I'm first
Soy el primero (boys)
Soy la primera (girls)
👄 soy el preemairo
   soy la preemaira

27

# Electronic games

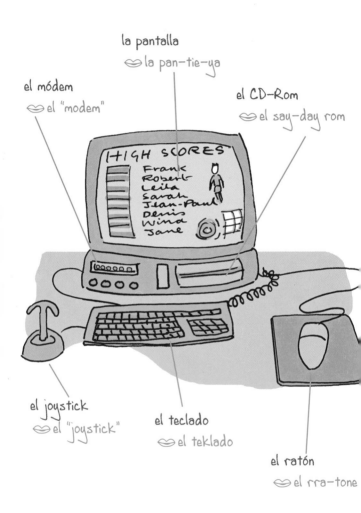

la pantalla
↪ la pan–tie–ya

el módem
↪ el "modem"

el CD–Rom
↪ el say–day rom

HIGH SCORES
Frank
Robert
Leila
Sarah
Jean–Paul
Denis
Wind
Jane

el joystick
↪ el "joystick"

el teclado
↪ el teklado

el ratón
↪ el rra–tone

What do I do?
¿Qué hay que hacer?
👄 kay eye kay asair

Show me
Enséñame
👄 ensay–nyamay

Am I dead?
¿Me han matado?
👄 may an
matado

Shoot-em-up!
¡Dispárales!
👄 deespa–ralayss

How many lives do I have?
¿Cuántas vidas tengo?
👄 kwantas beedas tengo

How many levels are there?
¿Cuántos niveles hay?
👄 kwantos neebay–les eye

# Non couch-potato activities!

tennis
el tenis
🗣 el tenees

trampolining
el trampolín
🗣 el trampoleen

bowling
los bolos
🗣 los bol-los

swimming
la natación
🗣 la nata-syon

hockey
el hockey
👄 el "hockey"

gymnastics
la gimnasia
👄 la heem-nasya

ballet
el ballet
👄 el ballay

basketball   el baloncesto
👄 el ballon-sesto

and, of course, we haven't forgotten *"el fútbol!"*

31

# soccer

**shoes**
las botas
👄 las botas

**shin-pads**
las espinilleras
👄 las espinee-yeras

**ref**
el árbitro
👄 el arbeetro

**soccer gear**
el equipo de fútbol
👄 el ekeepo day footbol

**Good save!**
¡Vaya parada!
👄 baya parada

**crossbar**
el larguero
👄 el largairo

**goalpost**
el palo
👄 el pallo

**Pass!**
¡Pasa!
👄 pasa

**goal**
el gol
👄 el gol

**goalie**
el portero
👄 el portairo

32

33

# Keeping the others in line

**Not like that!**
¡Así no!
👄 asee no

**You cheat!**
¡Tramposo! (boys only)
¡Tramposa! (girls only)
👄 tramposo
tramposa

**I'm not playing anymore**
Ya no juego
👄 ya no hwego

**It's not fair!**
¡No es justo!
👄 no es hoosto

**Stop it!**
¡No hagas eso!
👄 no agas eso

**Showing off**

Can you ...
¿Sabes ...
🔊 sabays

... do a handstand?
... hacer el pino?
🔊 asair el peeno

Look at me!
¡Mírame!
🔊 meera-may

... do a cartwheel?
... dar volteretas laterales?
🔊 dar boltair-retas latairal-les

... do this?
... hacer esto?
🔊 asair esto

## Impress your new friends with this!

You can show off to your new friends by practicing this tongue twister:

**Tres tristes tigres comían trigo en un trigal**

*trays treestays teegrays comee-an treego en oon treegal*

(This means "Three sad tigers ate wheat in a wheat field.")

Then see if they can do as well with this English one:

"She sells sea shells on the sea shore, but the shells she sells aren't sea shells, I'm sure."

# For a rainy day

**pack of cards**
una baraja de cartas
☞ oona baraha
day kartas

**my deal/your deal**
yo doy/tú das
☞ yo doy/too das

**king**
el rey
☞ el rray

**queen**
la reina
☞ la rray-een

**jack**
la jota
☞ la hota

**joker**
el komodín
☞ el komodee

tréboles
☞ trebol-les

corazones
☞ korason-nes

picas
☞ peekas

diamantes
☞ dee-amant

36

## Do you have the ace of swords?!

**Y**ou might also see children playing with a different pack of cards. There are only 48 cards instead of 52, and the suits are also different. Instead of clubs, spades, diamonds, and hearts, there are gold coins (***oros***), swords (***espadas***), cups (***copas***), and batons (***bastos***).

## chessboard
el tablero
⌣ el tablairo

el alfil
⌣ el alfeel

el peón
⌣ el pay-on

el rey
⌣ el rray

la reina
⌣ la rray-eena

la torre
⌣ la torray

el caballo
⌣ el kab-eye-o

37

hamburger
la hamburguesa
~ la amboorgaysa

fries
las papas fritas
~ las papas
freetas

ice cream
el helado
~ el elahdo

coke
una coca
~ oona koka

FEELING HUNGRY

38

squid
los calamares
👄 los kalama-res

caramel custard
el flan
👄 el flan

la paella
👄 la pie-eyya

orange juice
el jugo de naranja
👄 el hoogo day
naran-ha

# Grub

I'm starving
Tengo un hambre de lobo
👄 tengo oon ambray day lobo

That means "I have the hunger of a wolf!"

Please can I have ...
Por favor, me da ...
👄 por fabor, may da

... a cream pastry
un bollo con nata
👄 oon boyo kon nata

... a croissant
un cruasán
👄 oon krwasan

... a sweet roll
una palmera
👄 oona palmayra

... a bread roll
un bollo
👄 oon boyo

... a waffle
un wafle
👄 oon wah–flay

los churros
👄 los choorros

These are wonderful sugary doughnut-like snacks. They are sold in cafés and kiosks and, in Spain, they come in a paper cone. They are also very popular for breakfast in winter, with thick hot chocolate (**chocolate con churros**).

You: Can I have some churros, Mom?

Mom: No. They'll make you fat and ruin your teeth.

You: But I think it's good to experience a foreign culture through authentic local food.

Mom: Oh, all right then.

---

Churros? **"¡Mm, mm!"** Garlic sandwich? **"¡Agh!"** If you're going to make food noises, you'll need to know how to do it properly in Spanish!

"Yum, yum!" is out in Spanish. You should say **"¡Mm, mm!"** And "Yuk!" is **"¡Agh!"** (pronounced "ag"), but be careful not to let adults hear you say this!

# Drink up

I'm dying for a drink
Me muero de se...
🗣 may mwero day sed

I'd like ...
Me apetece ...
🗣 may apay–taysay

... a coke
... una coca
🗣 oona koka

... an orange juice
... un jugo de naranja
🗣 oon hoogo day naran–ha

... an apple juice
... un jugo de manzana
🗣 oon hoogo day mansana

In Mexico and other countries, the *limonadas* are carbonated. So instead of a plain lemonade, you're actually getting a lemon or lime soda-pop!

... a lemonade
una limonada
👄 oona leemo-nadah

... water
agua
👄 agwa

... a milkshake
... un batido de leche
👄 oon bateedo day laychay

You get your hot chocolate in a large cup (to dunk your churros in).

... a hot chocolate
... un chocolate
👄 oon chokolatay

## Did you know?

A lot of children have hot chocolate for breakfast in the morning and some of them will dip their churros or bread in it. They get very soggy and Mom is sure not to like this!

43

# How did you like it?

### That's lovely
*Eso está super bueno*
👄 eso esta soopair bweno

### That's yummy
*Eso está delicioso*
👄 eso esta daylee-see-oso

### I don't like that
*Eso no me gusta*
👄 eso no may goosta

### I'm stuffed
*Voy a explotar*
👄 boy a explotar

### I can't eat that
*No me lo puedo comer*
👄 no may lo pwedo komair

### That's gross
*Está asqueroso*
👄 esta askairoso

44

# Adventures in Eating!

If you're traveling in Mexico and Central America and you don't like hot, spicy food, a good question to know is **Es picante?** (*es peekantay*—"Is it spicy?"). If the answer is no, your tongue won't catch on fire!

And if you're hungry for comfort food, you can always ask for one of the following dishes:

noodle soup

sopa de fideos

👄 sopa day feeday-os

spaghetti

espaguetis

👄 espaghetees

... with meatballs

... con albóndigas

👄 kon albon-deegas

you can even ask for ...

pizza

pizza

👄 peessa

45

L
O
O**K**
**I**
**N**
**G**

**G**
**O**
**O**
**D**

nail polish
el esmalte para las uñas
el esmahltay para las oonyas

headband
la diadema
la dee-adema

bracelets
las pulseras
las poolsairas

braid
la trencit
la tren
seeta

crop top
la camiseta
la kamee

belt
el cinturón
el seen-tooron

miniskirt
la minifalda
la minee-fald

shoes
los zapatos
los sapatos

bike
la bici
la beesee

46

**spotted**
de lunares
 day loona-res

**flowery**
de flores
day flo-res

**frilly**
con volantitos
kon bolanteetos

**glittery**
con brillos
kon breeyos

**striped**
de rayas
day righ-yas

jeans
los vaqueros
👄 los bakayros

T-shirt
la camiseta
👄 la kameeseta

sweatshirt
la sudadera
👄 la soodadayra

tennis shoes
los deportivos
👄 los dayporteebos

dress
el vestido
👄 el baysteedo

pants
los pantalones
👄 los pantalone-nes

skirt
la falda
👄 la falda

soccer shirt
la camiseta de fútbol
👄 la kameeseta day footbol

shorts
los pantalones cortos
👄 los panta-lone-nes kortos

50

shoes
los zapatos
👄 los sapatos

# Color this page yourself
(you can't expect us to do everything!)

## colors
los colores
👄 los kolo-res

**white**
blanco
👄 blanko

**green**
verde
👄 berday

**orange**
naranja
👄 naranha

**blue**
azul
👄 asool

**pink**
rosa
👄 rossa

**yellow**
amarillo
👄 amareeyo

**red**
rojo
👄 roho

**purple**
morado
👄 morado

**black**
negro
👄 naygro

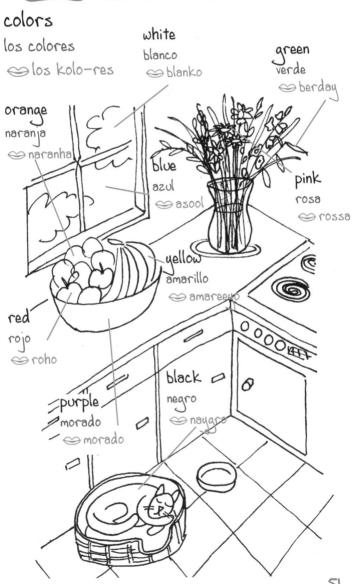

51

What should we do?

¿Qué hacemos?

👄 kay asay-mos

Can I come?

¿Puedo ir?

👄 pwedo eer

Where do you all hang out?

¿Por dónde salen ustedes?

👄 por donday salen oos-tedays

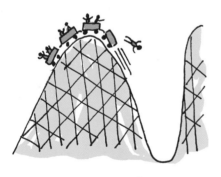

That's mega!

¡Qué emoción!

👄 kay aymosee-yon

I'm (not) allowed

(No) me dejan

👄 (no) may day-han

**Let's go back**
Regresemos
👄 regray-saymos

**That gives me goose bumps** (or "chicken flesh" in Spanish!)
*Eso me pone la carne de gallina*
👄 eso may ponay la karnay day gayeena

**I'm scared**
Tengo miedo
👄 tengo mee-aydo

**I'm bored to death**
Me muero de aburrimiento
👄 may mwero day aburree-mee-ento

**That's funny**
Te ríes cantidad
👄 tay reeyes kanteedad

55

# Beach babes

Can I borrow this?
¿Me dejas esto?
☞ may dehas esto

Let's hit the beac
¿Vamos a la playa?
☞ bamos a la playa

Is this your bucket?
¿Es tuyo este cubo?
☞ es tooyo estay koobo

You can bury me
Me puedes enterrar
☞ may pwedes entair-rar

Stop throwing sand!
¡Deja de echar arena!
☞ dayha day echar arayna

Watch out for my eyes!
¡Cuidado con mis ojos!
☞ kweedado kon mees ohos

56

sea
el mar
👄 el mar

beach
la playa
👄 la playa

nd castle
castillo de arena
👄 el casteeyo day arayna

towel
la toalla
👄 la toe-aya

bathing suit
el bañador
👄 el banyador

bucket
el cubo
👄 el koobo

snorkel
el tubo
👄 el toobo

shovel
la pala
👄 la palla

shells
las conchas
👄 las konechas

# It's going swimmingly!

*How to make a splash in Spanish!* →

PLOF

Let's hit the swimming pool
¿Vamos a la piscina?
👄 bamos a la peeseena

Can you swim (underwater)?
¿Sabes nadar (debajo del agua)?
👄 sabays nadar (debaho del agwa)

Me too/
I can't
Yo también/Yo no
👄 yo tambeeyen/
yo no

Can you dive?
¿Te sabes tirar de cabeza?
👄 tay sabays teerar day kabaysa

I'm getting changed
Me estoy cambiando
👄 may estoy kambee-ando

... backstroke
de espalda
👄 day espalda

Can you swim ...?
¿Sabes nadar ...?
👄 sabays nadar

... butterfly
a mariposa
👄 a mareeposa

... crawl
a crol
👄 a krohl

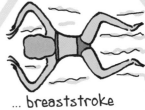

... breaststroke
a braza de pecho
👄 a brasa day paycho

slide
el tobogán
👄 el tobogan

goggles
las gafas
👄 las gafas

59

# Downtown

**Do you know the way?**
¿Sabes el camino?
👄 sabays el kameeno

**Is it far?**
¿Está lejos? 👄 esta lay-hos

## Pooper-scoopers on wheels!

In Spain you might see bright green-and-white motorcycles with funny vacuum cleaners on the side riding around town scooping up the dog poop. The people riding the bikes look like astronauts! (Well, you'd want protection too, wouldn't you?)

**Are we allowed in here?**
¿Nos dejan entrar aquí?
👄 nos day-han entrar akee

**Let's ask**
Vamos a preguntar
👄 bamos a pray-goontar

60

**playground**
el patio de recreo
🔊 el pateeyo day rekrayo

**slide**
el tobogán
🔊 el tobogan

**park**
el parque
🔊 el parkay

**swings**
los columpios
🔊 los koloom-peeyos

**bus**
el autobús
🔊 el owtoboos

**car**
el coche
🔊 el kochay

You can show off your "street smarts" to your new friends by using some slang.
A junky old car is **"una cafetera"** (*oona cafaytayra*), which means "coffee pot!" Try this: **"¡Vaya cafetera!"** (*baya cafaytayra*— "What an old clunker!").

61

# Picnics

**I hate wasps**
Odio las avispas
🗣 odeeyo las abeespas

**Move over!**
¡Apártate!
🗣 apar–tatay

**bread**
el pan
🗣 el pan

**Let's sit here**
¿Nos sentamos aquí
🗣 nos sentamos ak

**napkin**
la servilleta
🗣 la serbeeyeta

**ham**
el jamón
🗣 el hamon

**cheese**
el queso
🗣 el kayso

**yogurt**
el yogur
🗣 el yogur

**chips**
las papas fritas
🗣 las papas freetas

**drinks**
las bebidas
👄 las bebeedas

**knife**
el cuchillo
👄 el koocheeyo

**spoon**
la cuchara
👄 la koochara

**fork**
el tenedor
👄 el tenaydor

**wasps**
las avispas
👄 las abeespas

**bees**
las abejas
👄 las abayhas

bzzzzz

**ants**
las hormigas
👄 las ormeegas

# All the fun of the fair

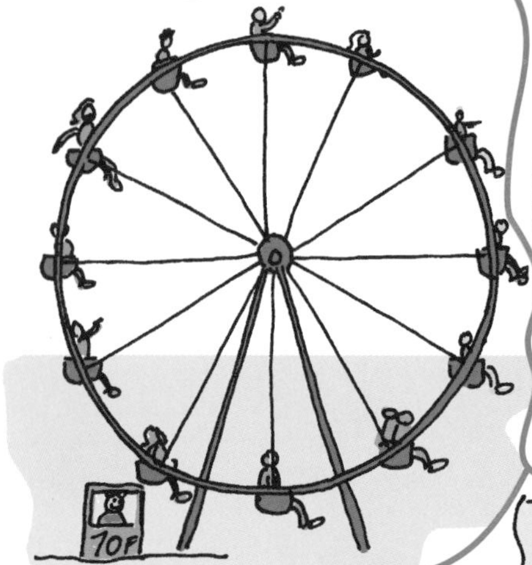

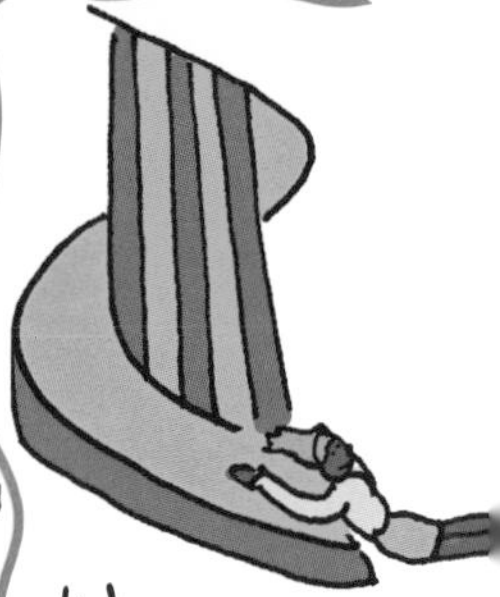

**slide**
el tobogán
🗣 el tobogan

**Ferris wheel**
la noria
🗣 la noreeya

**house of mirrors**
la casa de los espejos
🗣 la kasa day los espayhos

**bumper cars**
los coches de choque
🗣 los kochays day chokay

**Let's go on this**
¿Nos montamos en éste?
🗣 nos montamos en estay

octopus
el pulpo
👄 el poolpo

It's (too) fast
Va muy rápido
👄 ba mwee rapeedo

That's for babies
Eso es para los pequeños
👄 eso es para los pekay-nyos

WATER CHUTE

SPOOKY HAUNTED HOUSE

Do you get wet in here?
¿En éste te mojas?
👄 en estay tay mohas

I'm not going on my own
Yo solo (boys)/sola (girls) no me monto
👄 yo solo/sola no may monto

65

# Spend it here

**candy**
los caramelos
👄 los karamaylos

**T-shirts**
las camisetas
👄 las kameeseta[s]

**P O C K E T**

**M O N E Y**

**toys**
los juguetes
👄 los hoogaytays

**el tendero**
👄 el tenday[ro]

66

**books**
los libros
👄 los leebros

**mobile**
el móvil
👄 el mobeel

**pencils**
los lápices
👄 los lapeeses

POCKET MONEY

67

# What does that sign say?

Carnicería

carnicería
**butcher shop**
🔊 karneesereeya

pastelería
**cake shop**
🔊 pastele-reeya

Pastelería

confitería
**candy store**
🔊 confeete-reeya

panadería
**bakery**
🔊 panadereeya

Panadería

papelería
**office supplies**
🔊 papelereeya

Verdulería

PAPELERÍA

verdulería
**grocery store**
🔊 berdoole-reeya

## Money talk

Money has different names and values, depending on the country you visit.

boutique
**clothes store**
🔊 booteek

Boutique

Spain = **euros** (*ay-ooros*)
Mexico = **pesos** (*paysos*)
Guatemala = **quetzales** (*ketsalays*)
Costa Rica = **colones** (*kolonays*)

Of course, you must exchange your **dollares** (*doe-larays*) at a bank (**banco**—*banko*) or currency exchange (**casa de cambio**—*kasa day kam-beeyo*). But if you're in Puerto Rico, you're all set—the money is the same!

Do you have some cash?
¿Tienes lana?
👄 tee-enes lanah

I'm broke
No tengo ni un centavo
👄 no tengo nee oon sentahbo

I'm loaded
Estoy forrado
👄 estoy forrado

Here you go
Aquí tienes
👄 akee tee-enes

Can you lend me 100 pesos?
¿Me prestas cien pesos?
👄 may praystas seeyen paysos

No way!
¡Ni hablar!
👄 nee ablar

That's a bargain
Eso es una ganga
👄 eso es oona ganga

It's a rip-off
Es un robo
👄 es oon robo

69

# Sweet heaven!

### I love this shop
Me encanta esta tienda
👄 may enkanta esta tee-enda

### Let's get some candy
Vamos a comprar dulces
👄 bamos a comprar doolsays

### Let's get some ice cream
Vamos por un helado
👄 bamos por oon aylado

### lollipops
las piruletas
👄 las peerooletas

### a bar of chocolate
una tableta de chocolate
👄 oona tableta day chokolatay

### chewing gum
el chicle
👄 el cheeklay

If you really want to look cool, but end up with lots of fillings, ask for:

**regaliz**
(regaleess)

soft licorice sticks, available in red or black

**nubes** (noobes)

soft marshmallow candies in different shades (*nubes* means "clouds")

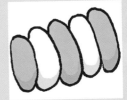

**jamones**
(hamon-nes)

fruity, fizzy gum in the shape of hams ("ham" is *jamón*)

**Chupa-chups®** (choopa-choops)

lollipops famous all over the world, but they come from Spain

**polvos pica-pica** (polvos peeka peeka)

tangy fizzy sherbet sold in small packets with a lollipop to dip in

**kilométrico** (keelomay-treeko)

chewing gum in a strip like dental floss—pretend to the adults that you're flossing your teeth!

# Other things you could buy
## (that won't ruin your teeth!)

**What are you getting?**
*¿Qué te vas a comprar?*
👄 kay tay bas a komprar

**That toy, please**
*Ese juguete, por favor*
👄 esay hoogaytay, por fabor

**Two postcards, please**
*Dos postales, por favor*
👄 dos postal-
les, por fabor

**How much is that?**
*¿Cuánto cuesta?*
👄 kwanto kwesta

**This is garbage**
*Esto es una porquería*
👄 esto es oona
porkayreeya

**This rules**
*¡Chévere!*
👄 chay-bairay

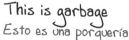

... colored pencils
... lápices de colores
👄 lapeesays day kolo-res

I'm getting ...

Voy a comprar 👄 boy a comprar

... stamps
... sellos
👄 seyos

... felt-tip pens
... rotuladores
👄 rotoolado-res

... a pen
... un boli
👄 oon bolee

... a cassette
... una cinta
👄 oona seenta

... a CD
... un compacto
👄 oon compacto

... comics
... tebeos
👄 taybayos

For many years Spain's favorite comics have been *Mortadelo y Filemón*, two accident-prone TIA agents (<u>not</u> CIA) and *Zipi y Zape*, two very naughty twins. Children also like to read *Mafalda*, an Argentinian comic, *Carlitos y Snoopy* (Charlie Brown & Snoopy), *Tintin*, *Astérix*, and *¿Dónde está Wally?* (Where's Waldo?).

Help!

Something has dropped/broken
Algo se ha caído/roto
💬 algo say a kigh-eedo/roto

Please
Por favor
💬 por fabor

Can you help me?
¿Me puedes ayudar?
💬 may pwedes ayoodar

Where's the mailbox?
¿Dónde está el buzón?
💬 donday esta el booson

Where are the toilets?
¿Dónde están los aseos?
💬 donday estan los asayos

I can't manage it
No puedo
🗨 no pwedo

Could you pass me that?
¿Me pasas eso?
🗨 may pasas eso

What time is it?
¿Qué hora es?
🗨 kay ora es

Come and see
Ven a ver
🗨 ben a bair

May I look at your watch?
¿Me deja que mire su reloj?
🗨 may deha kay meeray soo reloh

77

# Lost for words

... my ticket
mi billete
👄 mee beeyaytay

I've lost ...
He perdido ...
👄 eh perdeedo

... my parents
mis padres
👄 mees padrays

... my bike
mi bici
👄 mee beesee

... **my shoes**
mis zapatos

≋ mees sapatos

... **my money**
mi dinero

≋ mee deenayro

... **my sweater**
mi suéter

≋ mee swetair

... **my watch**
mi reloj

≋ mee reloh

... **my jacket**
mi chaqueta

≋ mee chakayta

# ADULTS ONLY!

**S**how this page to adults who can't seem to make themselves clear (it happens). They will point to a phrase, you read what they mean, and you should all understand each other perfectly.

No te preocupes
**Don't worry**

Siéntate aquí
**Sit down here**

¿Tu nombre y apellidos?
**What's your name and surname?**

¿Cuántos años tienes?
**How old are you?**

¿De dónde eres?
Where are you from?

¿Dónde te alojas?
Where are you staying?

¿Dónde te duele?
Where does it hurt?

¿Eres alérgico a algo?
Are you allergic to anything?

Está prohibido
It's forbidden

Tiene que acompañarte un adulto
You have to have an adult with you

Voy por alguien que hable inglés
I'll get someone who speaks English

uno    👄 oono

dos    👄 dos

tres    👄 trays

cuatro    👄 kwatro

cinco    👄 seenko

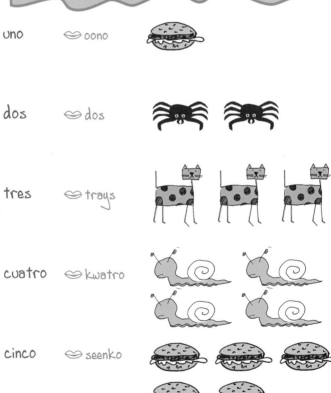

seis ⌣ sayis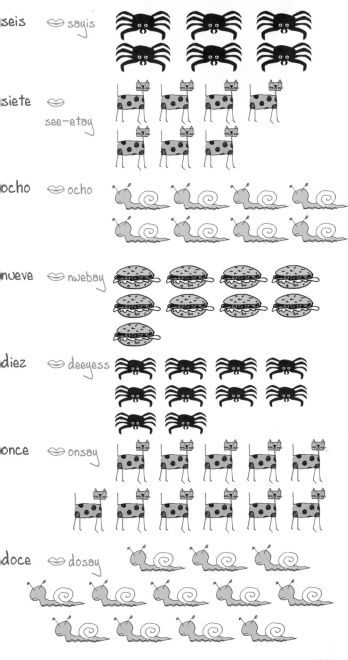

siete ⌣ see-etay

ocho ⌣ ocho

nueve ⌣ nwebay

diez ⌣ deeyess

once ⌣ onsay

doce ⌣ dosay

| 13 | trece | *tresay* |
|----|-------|----------|
| 14 | catorce | *katorsay* |
| 15 | quince | *keensay* |
| 16 | dieciséis | *deeyesee sayis* |
| 17 | diecisiete | *deeyesee see-etay* |
| 18 | dieciocho | *deeyesee ocho* |
| 19 | diecinueve | *deeyesee nwebay* |
| 20 | veinte | *baintay* |

I f you want to say "twenty-two," "sixty-five," and so on, you can just put the two numbers together like you do in English. But don't forget to add the word for "and" (**y,** pronounced *ee*) in the middle:

| 32 | **treinta y dos** | *traynta ee dos* |
|----|-------------------|------------------|
| 54 | **cincuenta y cuatro** | *seenkwenta ee kwatro* |
| 81 | **ochenta y uno** | *ochenta ee oono* |

| 30 | treinta | *traynta* |
|----|---------|-----------|
| 40 | cuarenta | *kwarenta* |
| 50 | cincuenta | *seenkwenta* |
| 60 | sesenta | *saysenta* |
| 70 | setenta | *saytenta* |
| 80 | ochenta | *ochenta* |
| 90 | noventa | *nobenta* |
| 100 | cien | *seeyen* |

| 1st | primero | *preemairo* |
| 2nd | segundo | *segoondo* |
| 3rd | tercero | *tersayro* |
| 4th | cuarto | *kwarto* |
| 5th | quinto | *keento* |
| 6th | sexto | *sexto* |
| 7th | séptimo | *septeemo* |
| 8th | octavo | *octabo* |
| 9th | noveno | *nobayno* |
| 10th | décimo | *dayseemo* |

## Want a date?

**I**f you want to say a date in Spanish, you don't need to use 1st, 2nd, etc. Just say the ordinary number followed by **de** (*day*):

| Lunes | Martes | Miércoles | Jueves | Viernes | Sábado | Domingo |
|-------|--------|-----------|--------|---------|--------|---------|
|       |        | 1         | 2      | 3       | 4      | 5       |
| 6     | 7      | 8         | 9      | 10      | 11     | 12      |
| 13    | 14     | 15        | 16     | 17      | 18     | 19      |
| 20    | 21     | 22        | 23     | 24      | 25     | 26      |
| 27    | 28     | 29        | 30     |         |        |         |

uno de marzo          (1st of March)

diez de Julio          (10th of July)

| March | marzo | *marso* |
| April | abril | *abreel* |
| May | mayo | *my-yo* |

| June | junio | *hooneeyo* |
| July | julio | *hooleeyo* |
| August | agosto | *agosto* |

| September | septiembre | *septee-embray* |
| October | octubre | *octoobray* |
| November | noviembre | *nobee-embray* |

| December | diciembre | *deesee-embray* |
| January | enero | *enayro* |
| February | febrero | *febrayro* |

87

primavera *preemabayra*

**SPRING**

verano *berano*

otoño *otonyo*

**FALL**

invierno *eenbee-erno*

| Monday | lunes | *loon-nes* |
| Tuesday | martes | *mar-tes* |
| Wednesday | miércoles | *mee-erkol-les* |
| Thursday | jueves | *hoo-ebes* |
| Friday | viernes | *bee-er-nes* |
| Saturday | sábado | *sabado* |
| Sunday | domingo | *domeengo* |

By the way, many kids have a two-and-a-half hour lunch break! Time enough for lunch and a siesta. But school doesn't finish until 5 o'clock!

# Good times

It's ...
Son ...
👄 sonn

(five) o'clock
las (cinco)
👄 las (seenko)

quarter after (two)
las (dos) y cuarto
👄 las (dos) ee kwarto

quarter to (four)
las (cuatro) menos cuarto
👄 las (kwatro) menos kwarto

half past (three)
las (tres) y media
👄 las (trays) ee medya

**five after (ten)**
las (diez) y cinco
👄 las (deeyes) ee seenko

**twenty after (eleven)**
las (once) y veinte
👄 las onsay ee baintay

**ten to (four)**
las (cuatro) menos diez
👄 las (kwatro) menos deeyes

**twenty to (six)**
las (seis) menos veinte
👄 las sayis menos baintay

W atch out for "one o'clock." It's different from the other times. If you want to say "It's one o'clock," you have to say **Es la una** (*es la oona*). "It's half past one" is **Es la una ee medya** (*es la oona ee medya*), and so on.

91

### morning
mañana
🗨 la manyana

### midday
mediodía
🗨 el medyo–deeya

### afternoon
la tarde
🗨 la tarday

### midnight
la medianoche
🗨 la medya–nochay

### evening
la noche
🗨 la nochay

# Weather wise

**Can we go out?**
¿Podemos salir fuera?
🗨 podaymos saleer fwera

**It's hot**
Hace calor
🗨 asay kalor

**It's cold**
Hace frío
🗨 asay freeyo

**It's a horrible day**
Hace un día horrible
🗨 asay oon deeya orreeblay

## It's raining seas!

In Spanish it doesn't rain "cats and dogs," it rains "seas!" That's what they say when it's raining really heavily:

¡Está lloviendo a mares! *esta yobeeyendo a ma-res*

## It's windy
Hace viento
👄 asay beeyento

## It's sunny
Hace sol
👄 asay sol

## It's snowing
Está nevando
👄 esta nebando

## It's raining
Está lloviendo
👄 esta yobeeyendo

## I'm soaked
Estoy empapado (boy)/
Estoy empapada (girl)
👄 estoy empapado/empapada

## It's nice
Hace buen tiempo
👄 asay bwen teeyempo

95

# Cheat Sheet

No
No
🗣 no

Yes
Sí 🗣 see

Hi!
¡Hola!
🗣 ola

Thanks
Gracias 🗣 graseeyas

Where?
¿Dónde?
🗣 donday

How much? ¿Cuánto?
🗣 kwanto

Please
Por favor
🗣 por fabor

Bye! ¡Adiós!
🗣 adeeyos